FOLLOW YOUR
Dreams

BY MO VAUGHN
WITH GREG BROWN
ILLUSTRATIONS BY CHRISTOPHER PALUSO

TAYLOR PUBLISHING
DALLAS, TEXAS

Greg Brown has been involved in sports for thirty years as an athlete and award-winning sportswriter. Brown started his Positively For Kids series after he was unable to find sports books that teach life lessons for his own children. He is the co-author of *Steve Young: Forever Young; Bonnie Blair: A Winning Edge; Cal Ripken: Count Me In; Troy Aikman: Things Change; Kirby Puckett: Be the Best You Can Be;* and *Edgar Martinez: Patience Pays*. Brown regularly speaks at schools and can be reached at pfkgb@aol.com. He lives in Bothell, Washington, with his wife, Stacy, and two children.

Christopher Paluso's sports illustrations have appeared on numerous magazine covers, plates, and prints. For five years, he provided the cover illustrations for *Legends Sports Memorabilia*, a leading sports collectibles magazine. Many of his plates, prints, and magazine covers have increased significantly in value over the years. Paluso is official artist for the San Diego Hall of Champions Sports Museum (he has painted all eighty-two members of the Hall of Fame) and the San Diego Holiday Bowl Hall of Fame.

Photos provided by Mo Vaughn and family unless otherwise noted.

Mo Vaughn has donated all of his royalties from the sale of this book to his Mo Vaughn Youth Development Program, which provides safe and constructive alternatives for inner-city youth that encourage them to care for themselves and their communities.

Special thanks to Frank Cantone and Mark Gillam. Without their interviewing and writing contributions, this book would not have been possible.

Designed by David Timmons

Published by Taylor Publishing Company
1550 West Mockingbird Lane
Dallas, Texas 75235

Library of Congress Cataloging-in-Publication Data

Vaughn, Mo, 1967–
    Follow your dreams / by Mo Vaughn, with Greg Brown and Mark Gillam, Frank Cantone; illustrations by Christopher Paluso.
        p.   cm.
    Summary: The first baseman for the Boston Red Sox uses his own life story to demonstrate the importance of staying focused on one's life goals.
    ISBN 0-87833-953-1
    1. Vaughn, Mo, 1967– —Juvenile literature. 2. Baseball players—United States—Biography—Juvenile literature. 3. Boston Red Sox (Baseball team)—Juvenile literature. [1. Vaughn, Mo, 1967– . 2. Baseball players. 3. Afro-American—Biography.] I. Brown, Greg. II. Paluso, Christopher, ill. III. Title.
GV865.V38A3   1996
796.357'o92—dc20
[B]   96-35565
                                  CIP
                                   AC

Printed in the United States of America
10 9 8 7 6 5 4 3 2 1

My name is Maurice Samuel Vaughn, but you can call me Mo. I play first base for the Boston Red Sox.

I've written this book to talk with you about the importance of following your dreams.

I believe everyone needs to have at least one dream. The dreams I'm talking about are not the nighttime kind. I'm talking about having hopes and goals.

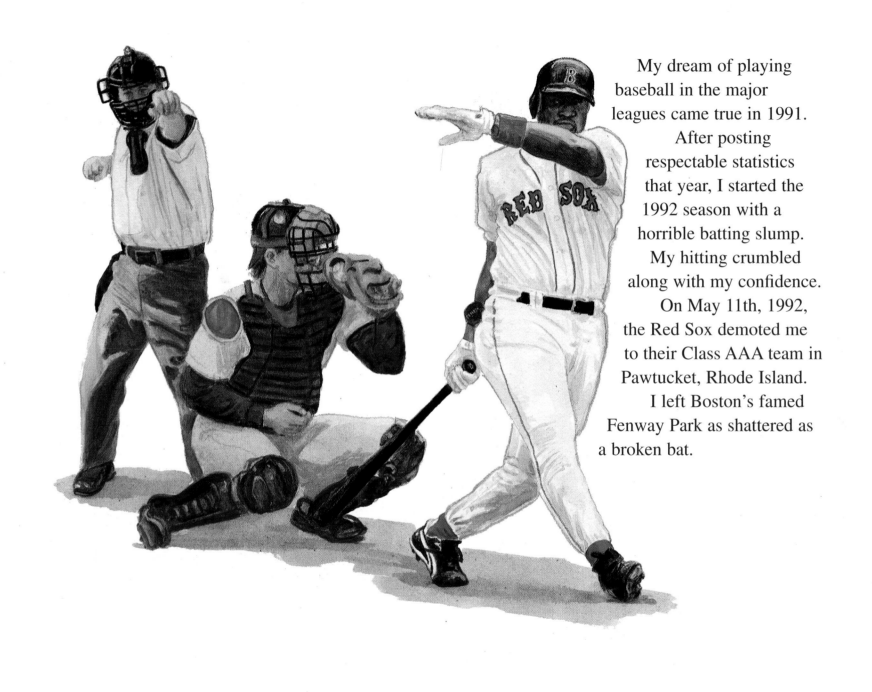

My dream of playing baseball in the major leagues came true in 1991. After posting respectable statistics that year, I started the 1992 season with a horrible batting slump. My hitting crumbled along with my confidence. On May 11th, 1992, the Red Sox demoted me to their Class AAA team in Pawtucket, Rhode Island. I left Boston's famed Fenway Park as shattered as a broken bat.

On my way back to
Pawtucket, I met my parents,
Leroy and Shirley, at a tiny
hotel.

That night was one of the
toughest of my life. I felt like
quitting the game.

Fortunately, my parents
talked me out of giving up.
They lovingly put their arms
around me and gently remind-
ed me to believe in myself,
just as they had done all along.
They said I would get another
chance if I worked hard and
followed my dreams.

By the end of our talk, I
knew I'd make it back to
Boston some day.

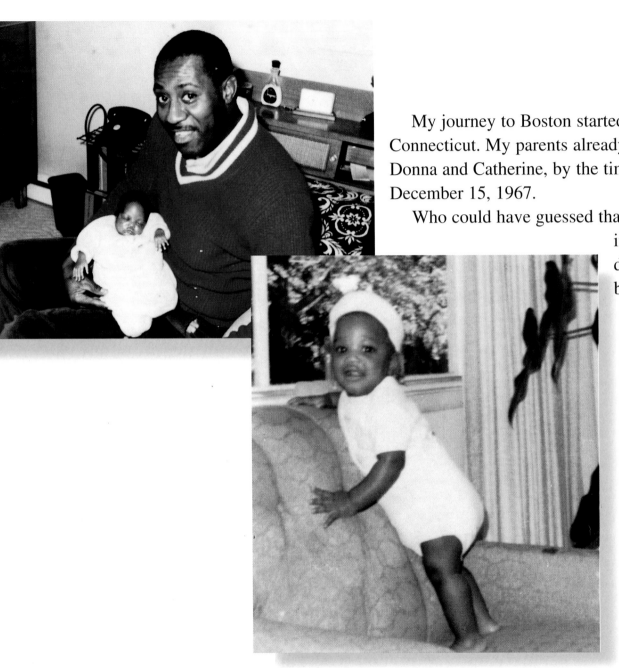

My journey to Boston started in Norwalk, Connecticut. My parents already had two daughters, Donna and Catherine, by the time I was born December 15, 1967.

Who could have guessed that tiny infant Dad held in his arms would one day be a professional baseball player?

Because my parents were both teachers (Dad eventually became a principal), education was important in our house.

Studying schoolwork and learning right from wrong went hand-in-hand with enjoying sports.

I discovered early I loved playing sports and tried my best to play them all.

Like all kids, I looked forward to Christmas. I remember one Christmas finding a set of drums next to the Christmas tree. I raced to them and immediately pounded away. (I went on to play drums in the school band in elementary and high school, and still play today. Those drums started my lifelong love of all kinds of music, with jazz and blues as my favorites.)

Opening presents gave us all joy, but my parents taught us that giving has its own rewards.

Every Christmas morning before opening our presents, our family would visit a homeless shelter.

Together we'd help cook and serve food, hand out gifts, and give words of encouragement to those who lost their dream or forgot how to dream.

That eye-opening Christmas tradition taught me many things. I learned I could talk with a variety of people. It made me thankful for my family, our home, and our blessings.

But most importantly, my parents' example showed that ambition needs to be balanced by compassion and caring for others.

Playing sports gave me opportunities to meet all sorts of people. I tried lacrosse, ice hockey, football, basketball, and baseball. I did well in all sports, even though I wasn't always the fastest or strongest.

Besides organized sports, I'd play sports in the neighborhood. My two older sisters were very protective of their little brother.

One day we were playing basketball near a street. The ball got away and I started to chase it. Donna shouted, "Don't run after it, you'll get hurt. I'll get it."

Donna ran into the street after the ball. She tripped and scraped her knee. She wasn't seriously hurt, but it showed how she always looked out for me.

During that time, I filled my room with posters of various athletes. One of my favorite basketball players was George Gervin, known as the "Ice Man." I had a poster that showed him on a block of ice. Now that was cool.

I'd stare at that poster and dream of playing pro basketball and someday being on a sports poster.

My parents strongly believed playing sports built character in people. My dad coached hundreds of kids over the years and was my baseball coach for several seasons.

I loved playing for my dad. He taught me the importance of trying my best all the time.

Mom had a hand in teaching me about sports as well. She instilled in me the belief that my dreams could come true.

In fact, Mom first taught me how to hit a baseball. Mom and I are natural left-handers, so when I was about three she started working with me in our backyard. She'd give me pointers and say, "Now, you hit that ball."

Later, we hung a baseball from a tree branch with a rope, and I'd hit that ball for hours.

To this day, Mom gives me advice on how to hit. And do you know what? She's usually right!

Although my parents were willing to help me improve athletically, they spent even more time guiding me with schoolwork and social skills.

Initially, I was a below-average student and sometimes a big bully in school. I made many trips to the principal's office during elementary school and junior high. Mom and Dad didn't work at the schools I attended, but they always found out when I got in trouble.

I went through times when I was disruptive in class and did not do my homework. Each and every time my parents would ground me, and I missed many events I wanted to attend.

The message didn't sink into my head until Dad made me learn a lesson the hard way.

After getting in trouble yet again, he yanked me off my junior high basketball team. I sat out the whole season.

I finally figured out trying my best in school and respecting others was easier than being in trouble all the time. I started spending countless hours studying. Math was most difficult for me and there were times I needed extra help from teachers.

Slowly, I began to understand. I have since grown fond of economics and use math all the time in my business life.

Background photo: Wendy Carlson

To make sure I concentrated on high school studies, my parents sent me to Trinity-Pawling School, an all-boys boarding school about forty-five minutes from my home.

I played football, basketball, and baseball four years for the Blazers. My freshman football season was probably the worst because we were 0-8. The season highlight came when one of my punts was blocked back into my hands, and I ran about 70 yards for a touchdown.

Mo's high school marks

- Earned twelve letters in football, basketball, and baseball
- Voted team captain in all three sports
- Earned a B average in the classroom
- Batted .465 last three years in baseball

I played running back, strong safety, and kicker.

Our basketball teams won three league championships with me playing forward.

Baseball, however, started taking over my dreams. Throughout the school year, I often would go out by myself and hit a ball off a cone into a fence. All those extra swings helped me hit .465 my last three years and average about six home runs a season.

You might be surprised to know I played mostly at shortstop in high school. One game I even saved a one-run win at shortstop by diving and catching a line drive to end the game with the bases loaded.

One high school accomplishment I'm proud of had nothing to do with sports. Every year six juniors are voted by their class and teachers at Trinity-Pawling to be the school leaders the next year. I was one of the six. I felt honored to have people think of me as a leader.

At the end of my senior year, a few colleges showed interest in me. Seton Hall University Coach Mike Sheppard offered me a baseball scholarship. Seton Hall has a tradition of sending players to pro ball, and since my girlfriend at the time also attended Seton Hall, I decided to be a Seton Hall Pirate.

Going to college was good for me in many ways. It opened my mind, and I matured. I made great friends on the baseball team and by joining the Omega Psi Phi fraternity. One of my fraternity brothers gave me the nickname "The Hit Dog."

Coach Sheppard gave me the nickname "Mo." He would always yell at me. "Maurice keep your eye on the ball. Maurice get your glove down. Maurice, Maurice, Maurice." Coach Sheppard shortened my name to Mo just to save time.

There were times when I hated Coach Sheppard screaming at me. I later realized he did it because he saw potential in me. Even though I had some God-given talents for baseball, I needed to build on those talents. For me, that meant working extra hard.

During fall practices my freshman year I hit only .093, so I knew I had to improve. I took as many swings as I could in the batting cage.

By spring, I became the designated hitter. My extra hitting paid off as I belted a school-record 28 home runs as a freshman.

Mo! Mo!

During that off-season, I set my goal to win the first base job.

Coaches told me I needed to improve my foot work around first base if I wanted the job.

I spent hours on a racquetball court during the winter with a radio, glove, bat, and rubber ball. I'd hit the ball off the wall at all different angles and catch it while listening to music.

I've found a secret to success is being willing to work hard even when nobody is watching.

The extra racquetball court practice gave me quicker feet and polished my fielding.

The next season, I became Seton Hall's starting first baseman.

I continued to prove I could hit the long ball my sophomore and junior seasons. I finished with 57 career home runs, which broke a Big East record. One time, I even hit a house with a home run ball. The field at Seton Hall has a short right-field fence 310 feet away from homeplate. There's a house beyond the bullpen about another 140 feet behind the fence. I cranked one out that hit the roof.

Coach Sheppard and his assistants helped me improve from the inside out. They reinforced what my dad taught me: To play the game right, you give your all, all the time.

Mo's Seton Hall Stats

Hit .417 during three seasons.
Belted school-record 57 home
    runs and drove in record
    218 runs.
Named to All-America team all
    three seasons.
Named Big East Conference
    Player of Decade.
Inducted into Seton Hall's Athletic Hall of Fame.
Smacked 28 home runs as freshman to break
    school's season and career records.

My hitting, fielding, and hustle earned All-America status three years, and I played on the USA All-Star team.

Boston picked me in the first round of the 1989 draft. It was a tough decision to leave college and my friends.

You will discover that life is full of tough choices. The best thing to do when making an important decision is to seek advice from people you respect.

I talked it over with everyone close to me and decided it was time for me to follow my dream to the next level.

Like most pro players, I had to work my way up through the minor leagues. My first stop was New Britain in Trenton, New Jersey.

There were a few scary moments in the minors. One game an infield throw hit me square in the face when I played for the Sox's Class AA team in New Britain. It was a routine ground ball. I covered first base to catch the infield throw, like always, but I turned and didn't see the ball coming. Luckily the blow didn't break my nose. I did have to leave the game with a slight concussion.

The next season, while at Class AAA Pawtucket, I broke my hand during a game. I continued to play, not realizing it was seriously injured until the next day. Broken hand and all, I got another hit.

Pain is part of the game of baseball. Getting plunked by a baseball hurts. If you expect never to be hurt playing sports, you'll probably be disappointed. The trick is learning to respect dangers while finding courage to overcome your fears.

Rich Dugas

In 1991 I received the call every minor leaguer dreams about. The Red Sox promoted me to the big-league club in Boston on June 27th.

Putting on the Boston Red Sox uniform for the first time was a proud day for me.

Things looked good that first season as I batted .260.

AP/Nick Wass

AP/Winslow Townson

I became the starting first baseman in Boston the next season, but a batting slump challenged my confidence the first month. I hit just .185 and managed only two home runs in our first 23 games. I felt pressure from all sides.

Fans booed and the media criticized. I felt as if I were sliding down a rope and couldn't hold on. I hit bottom when the Red Sox demoted me to Pawtucket.

As I mentioned, my parents boosted my spirits and helped me climb out of my depression.

Thanks to the encouragement from my family and the support of the Pawtucket fans, I knew I'd get another chance in the major leagues as long as I kept trying and swinging.

Jim Commentucci/Allsport

Five weeks after being sent down, I returned to Boston. My confidence was back, and I knew my career was off and running again.

Looking back, I can say my setback was one of the best things that ever happened to me.

Whenever I'm tired and need motivation, I think about the rough times I went through to reach the major leagues.

You can look at setbacks with bitterness or use them to make you a better person.

Former Boston hitting coach Mike Easler taught me how to channel my aggression into baseball.

Sometimes my bat feels like a lightning rod and all my power and emotions flow through it when I hit.

AP Photo

Fans love watching home runs, and I must admit hitting a home run is always a thrill. I can't hit baseballs over the fence whenever I want, so each one is special. Home runs make me think about all the swings I took in practice that made me a hitter.

I've hit many home runs that stand out in my memory. My first major league homer came three days after my debut. I belted it 438 feet and it almost went out of Baltimore's old Memorial Stadium.

One game in the Toronto SkyDome I hit the Hard Rock Cafe window, 430 feet away. And during a game at Yankee Stadium, I cracked a mammoth broken-bat blast into the upper deck and was left holding the splintered bat handle.

My most meaningful home run came in 1993 against the California Angels. Before the game I telephoned a young boy named Jason Leader, who was battling cancer. Despite his illness, he was in such high spirits that our talk inspired me.

I promised to try to hit a home run for him that night to celebrate his eleventh birthday.

Courtesy of the Boston Red Sox

My first two trips to the plate failed to produce a home run. When I went to bat a third time, Jason was in my thoughts. I got my pitch and delivered on my promise with a home run.

I got to know Jason better over the next few weeks, and was honored when he was able to throw out the first pitch to me in Boston.

Jason's courage touched everyone who met him.

My family has since participated in walk-a-thons to educate people about cancer and raise money for patients.

In 1994, I learned Jason passed away. I attended his touching funeral and felt proud to have known him.

Being part of others' dreams can be just as rewarding as following your own dreams.

One thing I enjoy doing is talking with kids. I visit schools to tell kids they can achieve anything if they earn respect through hard work, don't give in to peer pressure, don't do drugs, and stay in school.

The question kids ask the most is: "Do you love your job?"

I tell them nobody likes their job every day. That's why it's important to have balance in your life. That is one reason I try to help kids.

AP/Elise Amendola

I took about 250 kids to the Boston Ballet performance of the Nutcracker in 1993. I wanted to help them see the world in a new way.

We had such a great time that the next year I took 2,000 kids to see the Ringling Brothers Circus.

Those experiences led me to create the Mo Vaughn Youth Development Program in Dorchester, Massachusetts. It's a safe and positive place for kids to learn and spend time. I want kids there to know many people do care about them.

Despite my 6-1, 240-pound size and mean looks, kids bring out my soft side. I, too, still have some kid in me.

After playing night baseball games, I'm usually wound up from the game when I get home. To relax, I sometimes play video games. It relieves my stress.

Before I know it, I'll look up and it's three o'clock in the morning. Then I'm ready to sleep.

Playing video games to relax is one thing. Living to play video games is another.

If you find yourself spending more time playing video and computer games than anything else, that could keep you from following your dreams.

Another thing that kills dreams is holding on to the past.

Some might think they are jinxed by their family's situation or their background.

In Boston, some believe our team was jinxed by Babe Ruth.

After he was traded from the Red Sox to the New York Yankees following the 1919 season, some said Boston would never win a World Series without him. People call it the Curse of the Bambino.

I don't believe in jinxes or curses and you shouldn't either. You have to believe each day is a new chance.

You have to believe you can break patterns of defeat.

When people ask me how I think our team is going to do at the beginning of the season, I always say, "We're going all the way."

That's what I believe every season. Until the last out of the last game, I never give up hope. Thinking positively is an important step in making your dreams come true.

Babe Ruth
1895–1948
George Herman Ruth, nicknamed "Babe," still holds the record for most home runs by a left-hander (714) and most years leading the majors in home runs (12), among others. He had a lifetime .342 batting average. Although he is most remembered for his powerful swing that popularized the home run and saved baseball in the 1920s, in Boston (1914-1919) he was an outstanding pitcher with an 89-46 record.

My dream of playing in the postseason and winning a World Series became partly fulfilled during the 1995 season.

We ran away with the Eastern Division championship with an 86–58 record. The night we clinched the title ranks as one of my biggest thrills yet.

The pride earned by accomplishing a goal is something no amount of money can buy.

After the game, everyone at Fenway Park joined in celebrating our victory.

Roger Clemens hopped on a horse the police use for security and rode it around. He rode it to me and said I should ride it, too. Even though I was nervous about riding a horse for the first time, I jumped on and felt on top of the world.

AP/Winslow Thomson

AP/Winslow Thomson

Our celebrations ended when we met Cleveland in the playoffs. We lost three straight games. "Someone had to lose," is all I could say about it.

Cleveland fans dogged me for going hitless in the series. No matter what you do, there will be people who criticize you. The best way to answer is with positive actions. Success is the best revenge.

Failing to reach your dreams is always heartbreaking. My disappointment of losing to Cleveland lasted about a week before I started thinking about the next season and setting new goals.

Before the 1996 season started, however, I received a great honor. I was voted the Most Valuable Player of the American League for 1995. At the banquet, I received the award from a special lady, Rachel Robinson.

To receive the MVP trophy from her meant a great deal to me because her deceased husband, Jackie Robinson, was my favorite baseball player. Robinson played for the Brooklyn Dodgers and paved the way for people of color to play in major league baseball.

Robinson is the reason I wear No. 42. That was his number, too, and I wear it as a tribute to him.

AP/Osamu Honda

Jackie Robinson, 1919–1972

In 1947 Jackie became the first African-American to play in the major leagues. Jackie endured verbal abuse and many hardships and handled the pressure with poise and grace. He led the Brooklyn Dodgers to six World Series in ten years. He was named Rookie of the Year in 1947 and league MVP in 1949.

MVP Seasons Jackie's, 1949; Mo's, 1995		
Batting Ave	.342	.300
Home runs	16	39
RBI	124	126
Runs scored	122	98
Stolen bases	37	11

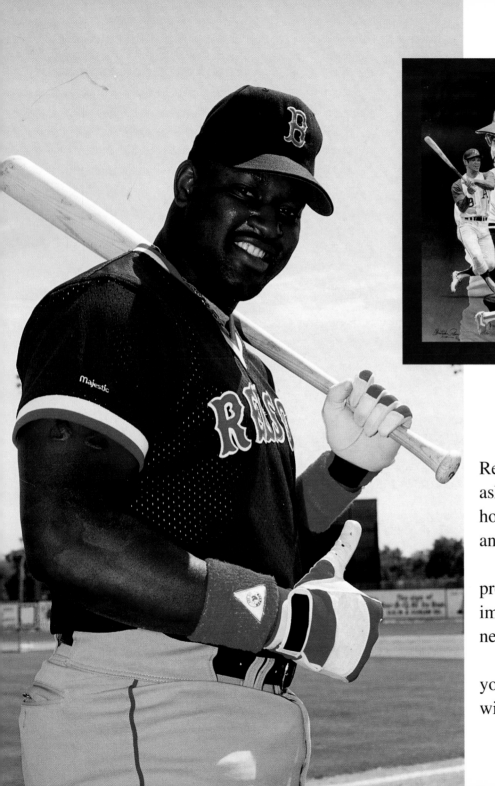

**Reggie Jackson
Born 1946**

Reggie, nicknamed Mr. October, earned two World Series MVP honors. He retired in 1987 with 563 home runs, sixth best all-time. He helped three teams win 11 division titles, six pennants, and five championships. Won American League MVP in 1973. Hit three home runs on consecutive pitches in '77 Series.

Recently, I sought out and met Hall of Famer Reggie Jackson. During our conversation, Reggie asked me an interesting question. He said, "Mo, how are you planning to become a better person and better ballplayer in the near future?"

His message was clear. Even though I'm a professional ballplayer, I still have room for improvement. And to improve in anything, you need a goal, a dream.

So shoot for the moon, and if you fall short, you're still a star. By following your dreams, you will go far.